HOW TO TURN YOUR EX-BOYFRIEND INTO A TOAD & OTHER SPELLS

ATHENA STARWOMAN
DEBORAH GRAY

HOW TO TURN YOUR EX-BOYFRIEND INTO A TOAD & OTHER SPELLS

For love, wealth, beauty and revenge

ATHENA STARWOMAN
DEBORAH GRAY

Illustrations by Sue Ninham

HarperCollins*Publishers*

HarperCollins*Publishers*

First published in Australia in 1996
Reprinted in 1996
by HarperCollins*Publishers* Pty Limited
ACN 009 913 517
A member of the HarperCollins*Publishers* (Australia) Pty Limited Group

HarperCollins*Publishers*
25 Ryde Road, Pymble, Sydney, NSW 2073, Australia
31 View Road, Glenfield, Auckland 10, New Zealand
77-85 Fulham Palace Road, London W6 8JB, United Kingdom
Hazelton Lanes, 55 Avenue Road, Suite 2900, Toronto, Ontario M5R 3L2
and 1995 Markham Road, Scarborough, Ontario M1B 5M8, Canada
10 East 53rd Street, New York NY 10032, USA
1160 Battery Street, San Francisco CA 94111

Library of Congress Cataloguing-in-Publication data not available at time of printing:

ISBN 0 7322 5709 3.

Cover and internal illustrations by Sue Ninham
Printed in Australia by Southbank Book

9 8 7 6   96 97 98 99

Dedicated to
whoever buys this book

This is the world's first interactive Magic book. Once you are the owner you will have activated its power. The Magic will remain energised by your unique, enchanted vibrations.

TOUCH HERE TO START THE MAGIC:

'In one hand she held the past,
in the other — the future'
— Bellthane, White Witch, 1664

'Believe in yourself
and in the absolute power of love'
— Athena Starwoman
and Deborah Gray, 1996

Contents

Introduction

The best witches always look fabulous

Yes, there are a few of us left who still insist on looking like Hippy Chicks — and we must admit, in the past, we ourselves have been guilty of wearing the odd feather and a few specially chosen love beads wrapped around a slim ankle. But now, all our gorgeous Witchy friends are using their Magic Powers and the Internet to cast their Spells, and they'd choose Chanel No. 5 over patchouli oil any day.

Whether we want to be lucky in love or to have great success in our careers, ever since Cleopatra won over Mark Antony, and Bathsheba conquered a nation, we girls have been stirring up plenty of Magic Potions and Enchantments to attract whatever we need and to give ourselves the best chance of success and happiness.

Magic can open our eyes to the wonder and
mysteries that surround us in our everyday lives.
So to help you get lucky in all aspects of your life,
we have put together a collection of the best and
most powerful Spells we know — Spells that
are fun and also easy to do.

Note: Many of the Spells specify a
particular phase of the Moon. Most New
Age stores can provide charts which
have this information.

THE BES

itches **ALWAYS** **OOK** **FABULOUS!**

Love & Sex Spells

A love goddess must have the right bedroom

We can't force anyone to love us — but we sure can help it along.
True love links us to the nature of the Universe and, with the right Magic
Spells and some good ol' feminine Witchery, we can all become
LOVE GODDESSES.

Love Goddesses are like the Best Witches — they always look
glamorous and they always have great bedrooms.

In fact, Witches invented glamour! The original Spellcasters would throw
'glamour' Enchantments all over themselves so that anyone who crossed
their path would be mesmerised by their beauty and fall madly in love.

Look for only positive and fulfilling relationships and remember that, for
the Magic to work, it's important to feel fascinating and intriguing.

CHAPTER I

The Perfect Soulmate Spell

For this Spell you will need these ingredients:

★

a clean white shirt
or dress

a box of gold glitter

a wooden stick
or pencil

Let's face it, we've all hungered for our 'perfect lover' at some stage in our lives. If you, like most of us, are still searching for your soulmate, then is this the Spell for you!

The best time to cast this Spell is on a clear night of a New Moon.

Begin by taking a bath or shower. Dress in your white clothes and, taking your box of gold glitter and wooden stick, go to a safe and secluded spot where you can easily look up at the stars in the sky. Find a bright star that appeals to you and take a few relaxing deep breaths to clear your mind of any stressful thoughts. Pick up your wooden stick, dip one end into the gold glitter and then raise the stick up towards your chosen star while you repeat these words aloud:

'With these Magic words
I begin my Spell.
Hear me, O mystic star,
Hear me well —
Let your Magic light
Send me the love of my life.
The Spell has been cast —
So Be It.'

Your gold glitter is now Magically energised and you should sprinkle some near the front door of your home. You can even take some out with you on your next social occasion and quietly drop a little around here and there.

Keep Your Lover Faithful Spell

For this Spell you will need these ingredients:

★

two pink candles

a bowl of spring or distilled water

a seashell

In the world of Magic there's an old saying that is a powerful Spell in itself: *You can't lose what is really yours.* However, if you want to make sure that your other half doesn't stray too far from your loving arms, try this Enchantment.

The best time to cast this Spell is on a Friday, at either 12 midday or 12 midnight, whichever suits you best.

Take a relaxing bath or shower and dry yourself thoroughly. Remain undressed and go to your bedroom and place all the ingredients on a table or flat surface and then seat yourself facing your Love Altar. Place the candles 30 cms (12 ins) apart and put the bowl of water and

seashell between them. Light the candles and then put the seashell into the water and, after clearing your mind of any negative thoughts, pick up the bowl and repeat these words:

'Oceana, Goddess of the seven seas, Keep my lover faithful to me — only me.'

Put the bowl back on the table and dab a little of the Magic water behind your ears and on your pulse points. Sprinkle some of the water around the bed you share with your lover. You could also offer to wash some of his clothes, and then put a few drops of the Magic water in with the wash.

If you plan to be away at any time, make sure you throw a drop or two of Magic water around the front and the back door of his and your home.

Hot Up Your Sex Life Spell

For this Spell you will need these ingredients:

★

a recording of your favourite, romantic love song

candles (optional)

two sticks of rose incense

some rose petals (fresh or dried)

a party mask

a soft scarf or some flowing material

your favourite perfume

a mirror

E ven Love Goddesses can sometimes run out of spark. But rest assured, this Spell has been tried and positively tested as a winner.

If your lover is willing, it would be great to include him in this hot Enchantment. He just needs to follow the same instructions, from beginning to end. If you wish, you can do it alone — it will still work wonders.

The best time to cast this Spell is on the night of a Full or a New Moon.

Prepare your bedroom by playing

romantic music softly and lighting candles or lowering the lights. Light the incense and throw some rose petals on your freshly made bed. Leave the mask and scarf on the bed while you have a luxurious bath or shower (preferably both of you, together).

Pat yourself dry and return to the bedroom. Stand skyclad (Witches' term for naked) in front of your mirror and slowly put on the mask. Wrap the scarf loosely around your hips. Take your perfume in your hand and dab on a few drops in three places — the throat, the chest and the stomach — while you repeat this Magic chant softly:

*'By the Magic
of Venus,
With the passion
of Eros,
I awaken the flame
of desire.'*

Now come close to your lover or to the mirror, and put the palms of your hands up in front of you while you say your lover's name out loud three times.

The rest is up to your imagination!

The Forget Me Not Spell

The best time to cast this Spell is on the night of a Full Moon.

Gather the Spell ingredients items together, and find a quiet spot in your home where you can be alone.

Place the white cloth on a flat surface and then put the mint, the photograph and your lover's underpants on top of the cloth.

Take a bath or shower and, after patting yourself dry, put on your own underpants and repeat this chant:

*'My love will protect you,
My love will
surround you,
You'll never forget my
love is true.'*

Now take off the underpants and place them with all the other items. Gather up the four corners of the cloth as if you're making a bag, then tie up the ends with the scarlet ribbon.

Keep your Forget Me Not bag in a safe place. Put it in your lover's luggage when he goes on a trip.

For this Spell you will need these ingredients:

★

*a square of white cloth
(a handkerchief will do)*

a sprig of mint

*a photograph of you
and your lover, together*

*a pair of your lover's
underpants*

*a pair of your sexy
underpants*

a piece of scarlet ribbon

The Marry Me Spell

For this Spell you will need these ingredients:

★

sandalwood incense

two pink candles

a cup of sand

an ochre- or brown-coloured lipstick

a piece of string, about 2 to 2.5 metres (about 6½ to 8 feet) long, wound into a ball

If marriage is on your mind, try this Spell on the night of a Full Moon.

Bring all the items of Enchantment into the bathroom and then take a relaxing bath or shower. After you have dried yourself thoroughly, remain undressed and light the incense and candles.

Sprinkle a handful of sand onto a table or a flat surface and then, with your index finger, draw a stick-figure in the sand while you are thinking of your loved one. Now smear the lipstick on your forehead in a circle shape, and take hold of the ball of string.

Hold the ball in the air, over the sprinkled sand, and then slowly unravel the string while you repeat this chant:

> 'Long string,
> make him love me.
> Long string,
> make him need me.
> Long string,
> make him marry me.'

Unravel the ball of string completely, until you have one long piece of string. Tie one end loosely around your waist. Dangle the other end of the string over the picture you drew in the sand, and concentrate on imagining your lover being drawn towards you, almost as if you were pulling him over to you with the string, and repeat the chant again.

When you have done this, roll up the string back into a ball and keep it in a safe and private place for as long as needed.

a LOVE *goddess* MUST have the RIGHT *bedroom*

The Romance Spell

For this Spell you will need these ingredients:

★

an item of green clothing

a wooden stick

a few peas (fresh or dried)

a cup of spring or distilled water

a flower

your favourite romantic novel

This Spell will help centre and prepare you for a long-lasting and romantic liaison.

The best time to cast this Spell is at midday on the first Sunday of the month.

Dress in something green, collect your ingredients, and go to a safe and private spot in a garden (or you could use a flower pot filled with earth).

Put all the ingredients around you and then seat yourself in front of a garden bed, near some fresh earth. Clear your mind of negative thoughts. Take the wooden stick in your hand, and draw a circle clockwise in the earth.

Take the peas, and bury them within the circle you have just drawn. Sprinkle a few drops of the water on top of the buried peas. After you have done this, place the flower on top of the sprinkled water. Stand and walk slowly clockwise around your Magic circle while you repeat this chant:

'Circle of Merlin
Around and above,
Water and earth
Bring me my love,
The circle is cast
The Magic will last —
So Be It.'

Take the flower from the centre of the circle and press it between the pages of the romantic novel for twelve days, until it has dried. You can then keep your Magic flower in a safe place, as your love charm.

The Dreamcatcher Spell

For this Spell you will need these ingredients:

★

a recording of your favourite love song

some floral incense

a bell

a feather

a piece of red material

This Spell will help you visualise your soulmate. It is said that once you have dreamt of your true love, he will appear soon after.

The best time to cast this Spell is on the first Thursday evening of the month.

Collect your Spell ingredients and find a light airy space where you can be alone. Place all of the ingredients on a flat surface or a table. Play the love song and sit comfortably in front of your Love Altar. Light the incense and clear your mind of stressful thoughts by breathing deeply and evenly for a few minutes. When the song is finished, pick up the bell and ring it three times. Then pick up the feather and wave it in the air near the incense smoke while you repeat this chant:

Wrap the feather up in the red material and, when you go to sleep that night, put it under your pillow.

'Keeper of my
dreams,
Bring me on the wind
My love to
embrace me.
Keeper of the night,
Let me see my heart's
delight.'

The Simply Irresistible Spell

For this Spell you will need these ingredients:

★

a piece of soft material, in pink or white

a small seashell (for sexual power)

a new key or one that has been washed in salty water

a hair from his head or a drawing of him

two sewing needles tied together with red cotton

some of your best spray perfume

a piece of white ribbon

This is a great Spell to make sure he finds you irresistible at all times.

The best time to cast this Spell is at midnight on a Full Moon.

Take all the items, except the piece of white ribbon, and place them on top of the piece of material. Close your eyes and imagine a beautiful golden light surrounding you, filling you with love and energy. Spray a little perfume over everything. Then gather up the four sides of the material so you make a small bag, and tie up the end with the ribbon.

Carry this Love charm with you whenever you feel the need. You can also keep it in a private place in your or his bedroom.

The Kiss Me Quick Spell

For this Spell you will need these ingredients:

★

gardenia-scented bath oil or bath salts

a mirror

a red candle

a stick of rose incense

a stick of musk incense

your favourite red- or pink-toned lipstick

If you'd like a man who just can't say no, try this Spell. Once he's kissed those Magic lips of yours, there'll be no turning back!

The best time to cast this Spell is on a Friday evening.

An hour or two before you meet up with your intended lover, take a long bath or shower with a few drops of the oil or bath salts. After drying yourself thoroughly, remain undressed and stand before your mirror. Light the candle and incense, then take your lipstick in your hand and draw the shape of a mouth on your mirror. Now picture your intended's face in your mind and imagine you see his face in the mirror — do this for at least thirty seconds. Now imagine that it's his lips that are on the mirror, and come as close as you can to that image and whisper these words.

Then get dressed in your sexiest outfit, and make sure you remember to wear your Kiss Me Quick lipstick.

'Lips of rose,
Lips so sweet,
My kisses are yours,
As soon as we meet.'

Bring Back My Love Spell

For this Spell you will need these ingredients:

★

two white candles

a photograph or a drawing of your ex-lover or friend (make sure he or she is alone in the photo — cover up or cut out anyone else in the picture)

a photograph of yourself smiling

a chamomile tea bag

a piece of blue material

This Spell can be used to bring back an ex-lover or to end an argument between friends.

The best time to cast this Spell is at precisely eight o'clock at night.

At exactly eight o'clock in the evening, light the candles and take a few deep breaths to relax you. Try to imagine a peaceful scene in your mind, perhaps a beautiful garden or waves rolling onto white sands. Now hold in your hand the picture of your ex-lover or friend, and repeat this chant:

> *'With the light*
> *of the flame*
> *I'll light your desire,*
> *When I speak your*
> *name*
> *You'll feel the glow*
> *from my fire.*
> *The Spell has been*
> *cast —*
> *So Be It!'*

Say his or her name slowly three times, and then put your picture face down on top of his or her picture so that the two images are together. Wrap up the two pictures, along with the chamomile tea bag, in the blue cloth. Put the package in a safe place.

To make sure your ex-lover or friend gets the message, light the candles at eight o'clock each night and repeat his or her name three times.

CHAPTER 2

Naughty Spells for Naughty Girls

(or how to turn your ex-boyfriend into a toad)

Don't get mad, get even

Even good little Witches find it necessary to partake in some delicious revenge. Nothing too drastic, of course — just enough retribution so that he never, ever, in his whole life, forgets that he hurt your feelings.

These Spells still come under the 'good' or 'white' Spell category because, after all, you are helping him in his spiritual growth — and **A REAL PRINCE CAN NEVER BE TURNED INTO A TOAD** (well, not for long anyway).

The Toad Spell

For this Spell you will need these ingredients:

★

a piece of cloth (one of his old shirts would be best)

a big handful of sandy dirt

a picture of your ex-boyfriend (or a drawing)

a darning needle

a piece of black thread

some green paint or a green felt-tip pen

If he's really done the dirty on you and run off with someone else, remember that in the larger scheme of things he's probably done you a favour. Nevertheless, this Spell will help others find him just as repellent as you do.

This is one of our favourite Spells and will prove to be most effective if done at midnight on a Full Moon.

Collect your ingredients and find a safe place where you can be undisturbed. Lay the piece of material on a flat surface. Put the dirt on top, and then the picture of your ex. Gather up the sides and then take the needle and thread and sew the material into a sack shape.

Take the green paint or pen and, on the outside of the bag, draw the ugliest toad you can.

Leave it under the Moonlight for the whole night. In the morning, throw the lot into the garbage bin.

He Just Can't Have Fun Without You Spell

Hey, you don't want to rain on his parade — but should he be really be having that much fun without you?

This Spell is to be used when you're really ready to let go of any attachments, especially to him.

The best time to cast this Spell is at

For this Spell you will
need these ingredients:

★

*a piece of clothing that
belonged to him —
except, of course,
anything that still looks
good on you; if you can't
find anything, write down
his name on a large,
clean piece of paper*

a ham bone

a plastic bag

some string

*a large plastic
container (big enough
to take the ham bone)*

three cups of salted water

ten o'clock on a
Saturday night.

Take the object
you've chosen (or the
piece of paper) and
wrap it around the ham
bone. Then put the
wrapped bone in the
plastic bag and tie up
the end with the string.

Put the package
into the plastic
container, pour in the
salted water, and
cover with a lid. Let

stand, where it won't
be disturbed, for
seven days.

On the following
Saturday, at ten
o'clock in the
morning, take the
plastic bag out of the
container. Remove
the plastic bag, wrap
up what's left in
newspaper, and bury
the parcel in the
ground away from
your house.

The Cool-Down Spell

For this Spell you will need these ingredients:

★

a piece of paper

a plastic container

some water

a piece of fish

a refrigerator freezer

This Spell is especially good for freezing out pesky ex-girlfriends. You know the one that he keeps mentioning with glowing praise and a special gleam in his eye? Yes, well, if you've been looking longingly through jewellery shop windows and she's definitely *not* on your wedding-guest list, this Spell should do the trick.

For this Spell to work, you'll need to find out her full name.

The best time to cast this Spell is on the night of a Full Moon, preferably at midnight.

Write her full name on the piece of paper. Roll the paper into a ball and put it into the plastic container along with the water and the fish. Then put it all in the freezer compartment of your fridge, in a place where you know it won't be disturbed or found (especially not by your boyfriend).

Leave it there for as long as it takes.

The Good Riddance to Bad Rubbish Spell

For this Spell you will need these ingredients:

★

a wooden clothes-peg (to make a peg doll)

some black ink or a black felt-tip pen

a small piece of the person's clothing or a picture of that person

some black thread

a pin

some black pepper

This Spell can be used to get rid of anyone who is bothering you, especially troublesome ex-boyfriends.

The best time to cast this Spell is on a Saturday.

Collect the items together and go to a safe and secluded

room in your home. Lay all the items around you. Chant these words:

'This Spell I do within
my rights to be free,
Darken my house
no more.
Begone [say the
person's name],
Begone from me!'

To make the doll, paint the peg with the black ink and then wrap the picture or material around it and tie with the piece of cotton.

Sprinkle the wrapped doll with pepper, and then pick up the pin and stick it into the peg doll as you repeat the chant.

Bury the doll near the front door of your home.

To Break a Hex Spell

For this Spell you will need these ingredients:

★

a sprig of rosemary

a piece of yellow paper

a red pen

scissors

a red cloth

paprika or red pepper

a piece of red cotton

If ever you feel that someone is putting negative energy or a curse on you, this will break the Spell.

The best time to cast this Spell is midnight on a Saturday.

While you are performing this Spell carry some rosemary with you at all times.

Write the person's name on the piece of yellow paper. If you're not sure of the name of the person who's placing the curse on you, just right down the words 'enemy mine'.

Using the red pen, draw a figure or a doll shape around the name and then cut out the shape with your scissors. Lay the paper doll face down on the red cloth and sprinkle it with the paprika. Tie the red cotton around the middle of the paper doll and then wrap it up in the red cloth.

Hold the wrapped up doll in your hand tightly and repeat these words:

'Enemy mine your
    power is gone
The hex is broken
The Spell is undone
The eye has been
    turned away.
Enemy mine you've
    gone away
So shall it be from
    this day.'

Perform this Spell for seven consecutive nights at midnight. On the next Sunday unwrap the paper doll and tear it into nine pieces, and then burn it. Scatter the ashes far away from your home, and throw the remaining red cloth into the garbage.

The Noisy Neighbour Spell

For this Spell you will need these ingredients:

★

a yellow candle

a teaspoon of salt

half a cup of olive oil

a chicken feather

If you'd like someone to move out of your neighbourhood, try this Spell at sunset on the eve of a New Moon.

Collect the items together, and go to a quiet area in your home where you can be alone. Light the candle and put the salt into the cup of olive oil. Pick up the feather and repeat these words:

'Cauda Draconis,
Help me in my time
of need.
I want [say the
person's name]
To move away from me.'

Dip the feather into the olive oil and, as soon as you are able, wipe the feather on the ground in front of your house and near your neighbour's house (make sure nobody sees you).

The Jealousy & Gossip Spell

For this Spell you will need these ingredients:

★

a yellow candle

scissors

a small stuffed toy or doll (one that you have purchased for this Spell)

some slippery elm powder (available from health-food stores)

a black cloth

When someone's been spreading rumours or speaking badly about you, this will help.

The best time to cast this Spell is on a Saturday, at eight o'clock in the morning or evening.

Place all the items in front of you on a flat surface and light the yellow candle. Think about the person who's been spreading the rumours, and say his or her name out loud three times. Now take

the scissors and snip a hole in the mouth of the toy. Pour the slippery elm powder into the hole and then blow out the candle. Put a few drops of wax into the hole as well.

Wrap the toy up in the black cloth and repeat these words:

'Who dares to lie
about me
Shall feel my wrath
abound
No-one listens and
I am set free —
So Mote It Be.'

If you know where your enemy lives, bury the toy near his or her home. If not, put it in a garbage bin far away from your house.

The Mother-In-Law Spell

This Spell is very useful to guard you against just about anyone that you have a personality clash with — but especially your in-laws.

The best time to cast this Spell is on the evening of a New Moon.

Using a mortar and pestle or a wooden bowl and spoon, mix the passionfruit seeds, rosemary, thyme and saffron in a container and grind them all into a powder. Inscribe the person's initials into the candle with the clean nail, then light the candle and repeat these words:

'In the name of Raphael and Gabriel, I beseech thy divine help in furtherance of my petition. Bless this candle — may my words find friendly ears.'

Let the candle burn for one hour and then take the herbal mixture and bury it in the potted earth of the violet plant.

When you are ready to open up the lines of communication, give the plant as a gift to the disagreeable party.

For this Spell you will need these ingredients:

★

a mortar and pestle or a wooden bowl and spoon

a teaspoon of passionfruit seeds (dried in the sun)

a teaspoon of rosemary leaves

a teaspoon of thyme leaves

a teaspoon of saffron threads

a Sweet Violet or African Violet in a pot

a white candle

a clean nail

The Break-Up Spell

For this Spell you will need these ingredients:

★

a dark blue candle

a blue pen

a piece of paper that he's written on or touched

a pair of sexy undies

an ashtray

a teaspoon of peppermint tea leaves

A bit of healthy competition can be good for all of us, especially in the game of love. If your intended lover has eyes for you but that girlfriend of his keeps getting in the way of your happiness, then try this Spell.

The best time to cast this Spell is at the stroke of midnight on a Saturday.

Collect the items together and find a quite place where you can be undisturbed. Gather the items around you. Light the candle, and take a few deep breaths to relax.

Then take the pen and write his name on one end of the paper and the girlfriend's name on the other. Tear off the end of the paper where you've written his name, wrap it up in a pair of your underpants, and put it under your bed.

Put the other piece of paper with the girlfriend's name on it into the ashtray, and sprinkle a little of the peppermint over it. Now, burn the paper in the ashtray and repeat these words:

> 'Only love that's deserved shall be,
> With me he shall remain —
> So Mote It Be.'

When the paper has completely burned to ashes, wait till it has cooled and throw it out of your window as far as you can.

Money & Success Spells

CHAPTER 3

Money will come when you are ready to receive it

Now that you're good and ready to receive your wealth, we can remind you that true wealth is to be found in your own inner peace and happiness. That doesn't mean, however, that you have to avoid money and live a cloistered existence. **REAL WITCHES HAVE NEVER GONE IN FOR SACKCLOTH,** and sleeping on beds of nails has never been on a true *Love Goddess*'s agenda. Letting go of the need for attachments is the key here — we never really own anything anyway, we just borrow it for the time that we need.

The Rich Witch Spell

For this Spell you will need these ingredients:

★

a teaspoon of cinnamon

a teaspoon of nutmeg

a bowl and spoon

three coins of low denomination

an old purse or wallet (one that you don't use any more)

This Spell should help to increase the bank balance. The best time to cast this Spell is on the evening of a New Moon.

Gather the ingredients together and find a private place. Put all the items on a flat surface in front of you. Seat yourself comfortably. Then put the cinnamon and nutmeg into the bowl, and mix with the spoon. This mixture will become your Attraction Powder.

As you mix the Attraction Powder, imagine a specific amount of money that you'd like to see in your bank account. Think big but don't go overboard and be greedy or you'll scatter the Spell's energy. You need to focus on that amount while you take the coins in your hand and throw them until you get one tail and two heads.

Put the coins and the Attraction Powder together into the purse and shake it up while you repeat these words:

'Attraction Powder
let it be
Send me all the
luck I need.'

Put the purse in the same place as you keep your money documents.

The Money Magnet Spell

For this Spell you will need these ingredients:

★

two white candles

a magnet

a cup of spring or distilled water

This Spell will help attract success in all your business dealings.

The best time to cast this Spell is on the evening of a New Moon.

Lay all the items on a flat surface and light the candles. Clear your mind of any negative or stressful thoughts, and try to focus on what you would like to achieve in the next year or so. Think about where you'd like to see yourself — perhaps in a brand-new house, or driving that little red sports car you've had your eye on, or in a plush new office and heading a corporation. Whatever you think of, keep it pictured in your mind for a minute or two. Then pick up the magnet, place it into the cup of water, and repeat these words:

'Artemis, Luna
magnified by thee,
Bring me success —
O Blessed Be.'

Put out the candles. Take the magnet and the cup of water, and stand near your front door. Sprinkle a few drops of the Magnetised Water on your door handle, and put the rest of the water in with the next clothes wash.

Carry the magnet with you in your wallet at all times.

Lucky Lottery Spell

For this Spell you will need these ingredients:

★

a small piece of putty or Plasticine

some gold paint (or gold eyeshadow or gold lipstick)

a small paintbrush

a piece of green string or cotton

a pen and paper

To give you good luck when you're picking winning lottery numbers, try this Spell.

The best time to cast this Spell is at nine o'clock on a Thursday evening.

Put all the items on a table. Rid yourself of negative thoughts and take the piece of putty or Plasticine and roll it into a small ball in you hand. Now press your right thumb into the ball to flatten it and then, using the paintbrush, put a dab of the gold paint on the thumbprint. To make your Seal of

Jupiter, wrap up the ball with the green string and repeat these words:

'Seal of Jupiter
— tied to me
give me numbers on a
count of three.'

Clap your hands three times and then write down any numbers that come into your mind.

Keep the Seal of Jupiter and your lucky numbers in with your money documents and use them whenever you need lucky numbers.

Be a Winner Spell

For this Spell you will need these ingredients:

★

a piece of white cardboard or stiff paper (large enough for you to sit on)

a blue pen

To help you win that deal, or for success in a new venture — you can create a Winner's Circle and use it whenever you like.

The best time to cast this Spell is on a Monday night at seven o'clock.

Begin by taking a bath or shower. After drying yourself thoroughly, remain undressed and go to a private room in your home where you will be undisturbed. Put the piece of cardboard on the floor and draw on it a large circle in a clockwise direction with the blue pen. Then stand within the circle, raise your arms into the air and take a few deep breaths. After you have done this, seat yourself in the centre of the circle and repeat these words:

'By the power of the number,
By the power of Fortuna,
All who sit within this circle
Shall prosper.'

Now write the numbers 7, 11, 9 on the cardboard and finish off with these words:

'The circle is cast,
The Magic will last —
So Be It.'

Keep the Winner's Circle in a safe place and sit in it whenever you have to make a business decision.

Getting that Job Spell

For this Spell you will need these ingredients:

★

a blue item of clothing

a silver candle

some lavender

a teaspoon of saffron

a teaspoon of rock salt

half a cup of sand

a small box

Whether you want a promotion or you're looking for a new job, this Spell should help.

The best time to cast this Spell is on a Monday at seven o'clock in the evening.

Begin by taking a shower or a bath, and then get dressed into something blue. Make yourself comfortable in a private space and lay all the items on a flat surface in front of you. Sit down and relax your mind and body for a few minutes. Light the candle and repeat this chant:

*'I open my heart
to receive the love
of the Universe,
Show me the way to
success and wisdom.'*

Now mix the lavender, saffron, salt and sand together thoroughly. Then throw a little out the window and around your home or work-place. Keep the rest in the box and, if you're looking through the newspaper for a job, sprinkle some over the employment section.

When you go on an important interview, wear something blue and carry some of the Magic mixture with you.

Money WILL COME WHEN *I'm* READY TO RECEiVE IT

The Born to Shop Spell

For this Spell you will need these ingredients:

★

two green candles (to symbolise money)

two pieces of clean white paper

a green pen or pencil

a coin of high denomination, washed clean in salty water

For the girl who wants everything, this Spell is really effective when you focus on one particular item or amount of money at a time. There's sure to be something you'd like to purchase but it seems out of your reach right now. Well, stop thinking that way — with this Enchantment, you'll be surprised at what happens when you know what you really want.

The best time to cast this Spell is on a Monday night at nine o'clock.

Gather the ingredients together and find a quiet room or space where you can take a few minutes to meditate and clear your mind. Light the candles and think about what you need and visualise it in your mind while you repeat these words:

> 'With a clear mind and
> an open heart
> I walk towards my goal.'

Imagine yourself walking towards a golden light in which you see the object of your desires, and then write down the amount of money you need or the name of the item on both pieces of paper. Wrap one piece of paper around the coin and keep it near your banking documents. Keep the other piece of paper near your bed so it's one of the last things you see before you go to sleep each night.

Break the Casino Spell

For this Spell you will need these ingredients:

★

chamomile tea

a favourite crystal (New Age stores have special ones to attract luck and money)

two new dice

a green velvet cloth

a piece of gold thread or string

Try this Spell if you are planning a trip to a casino. Witches love to have fun in the games of chance, but the Witches' secret to successful gambling is to do it only occasionally and *never* risk income that they can't afford to lose.

You can only gamble with funds that you don't really need. This is the fundamental rule to money Magic.

The best time to cast this Spell is at seven o'clock in the evening.

Make a pot of chamomile tea and wait till it cools down and then put it in the fridge for half an hour. Pick up the crystal and clear your mind of stressful thoughts and then repeat these words:

'Bring me silver,
Bring me gold,
Bring me money
hot or cold.'

Put all the other items on a flat surface and then throw the dice until you get two sixes. Now take out the cold chamomile tea and put the crystal and the two dice into the tea then dip your fingers into it as well. After this, take out the crystal and dice, dry them and place them on the piece of velvet and tie up the ends with the gold thread. Take the lucky pouch with you, and good luck!

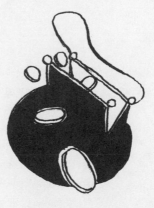

The Four-Leaf Clover Spell

For this Spell you will need these ingredients:

★

a four-leaf clover (if you can't find one, you can make your own)

this book

This Spell will help attract positive energy and good luck into your life.

The best time to cast this Spell is on the evening of a New Moon.

(To make your own four-leaf clover, draw the shape of a four-leaf clover on a piece of paper, colour it in with green paint or a green felt-tip pen. When the paint or ink is completely dry, cut out the shape with scissors.)

Lay the four leaf clover on this page of

the book so you can energise it with Athena and Deborah's Magical energy. Put your right hand on top of the page as well, and feel the Enchanted energy warming your hand. When you are ready, close the book and leave it in a safe place for twenty-four hours.

The next day open the book, take out the energised four-leaf clover and carry it with you whenever you feel the need for positive energy and good luck.

The Real Estate Spell

For this Spell you will need these ingredients:

★

a stick of sandalwood incense

a teaspoon of mint

a teaspoon of golden seal powder (available from health-food stores)

a teaspoon of nutmeg

a bowl

a small wooden stick or pencil

This Spell is very effective if you want to sell or buy some property.

The best time to cast this Spell is on a Thursday evening.

Gather all your ingredients and find a private spot in your home. Light the incense and leave it to burn until only the ashes are left. Wait till it completely cools, and then collect the ashes in the bowl. Using the wooden stick, thoroughly mix the ashes with all the other ingredients.

If you want to sell your home, sprinkle a little in every corner of the house or apartment. If you'd like to buy a property, put a little of the mixture into your right shoe when you go looking.

The Lucky Dog Spell

For this Spell you will need these ingredients:

★

half a teaspoon of salt

a small box (an empty matchbox will do fine)

a hair or two from a dog

a pinch of basil

We like to be around as many lucky dogs as we can, in the hope that some of their good luck rubs off on us. But just in case they're in short supply, you can have your own personal Lucky Dog Amulet to bring you lots of success in all your business and money dealings.

The best time to cast this Spell is on the evening of a New Moon.

Gather the Spell ingredients together and go to a private place where you can be alone. Place all the ingredients on a table or flat surface, and then seat yourself comfortably nearby. Close your eyes and relax your body. Take a few, deep, even breaths to clear your mind. Open your eyes. Take a pinch of salt in you right hand and throw it over your left shoulder while you repeat these words out loud:

'With the Salt of the Earth
The Magic begins.'

Now put the rest of the salt into the box, along with the hair of the dog and the basil, and repeat these words:

'By the hair of the dog
By Luna, by Time
The Magic is cast —
So Be It.'

Carry the Lucky Dog Amulet with you whenever you attend an important business meeting or when you want to attract money towards you.

CHAPTER 4

Me, Me & I Spells

What you think, you become

Girls just want to have fun!

If you're already so popular that everybody hates you, you probably don't need social skills. But most of us usually find that being the centre of attention wherever we go is not only desirable but a downright must.

WHAT YOU THINK, YOU BECOME. Let go of negative and defeatist thinking. If you project a feeling of wellbeing and happiness, you will find other people reacting that way towards you. These Spells will help you cast away all those barriers that can come between yourself and all the fun you deserve to have.

The Party-Girl Spell

For this Spell you will need these ingredients:

★

an empty notebook (keep the notebook as your Magical Diary)

a blue pen

With this Spell, life's a party and you're invited!

The best time to cast this Spell is on the eve of a New Moon.

Collect the items and find a quiet place where you can be undisturbed for at least half an hour.

Place the notebook and pen on a table and seat yourself comfortably nearby.

Close your eyes and, after take a few deep breaths, imagine that you see a white light surrounding you. Feel this white light calming you and filling you with happiness.

Now think of something that you'd really love to do in your spare time, perhaps taking a holiday or going to a great party or meeting some new and interesting people.

After you have chosen one social activity that appeals to you, write down a description of the event in your notebook. Look carefully at whatever you have written down and then draw the shape of a square (almost like a doorway) around it.

Now, imagine that you are opening this door and you are stepping through it. In your mind's eye imagine that you have arrived at the social event or holiday that you wished for. 'See' and sense it happening around you, and repeat these words:

'To the left and right of me
Above and below me
I awaken the spirit of
Nature within me.'

When you feel energised and ready to return, close the notebook and try to carry with you that same great feeling.

I'm a Great Artist Spell

For this Spell you will need these ingredients:

★

some peppermint tea

a mirror

a scarf made of natural material

a red lipstick or crayon

How would you like to get a few tips on painting from Leonardo da Vinci, perhaps have a chat with Mozart on the joys of music, or learn from Elvis and Marilyn how to swivel your hips? When you really understand what Magic is built on — the fact that all energy is connected — then, any time you'd like a shot of inspiration, you can try this Spell.

The best time to cast this Spell is at seven o'clock in the morning or evening.

Make the peppermint tea and breathe in the aroma for a moment or two.

Put all the items of Enchantment on a flat surface in front of the mirror, and seat yourself in a relaxed position where you can see your reflection.

Drape the scarf around your shoulders. Take the lipstick or crayon and draw a large circle on the mirror while you recite these words:

*'The circle is cast,
Only the good can
enter herein.'*

Now write the name of the great artist you'd like to connect with, in the middle of the circle, and write your name underneath the artist's name. Then look directly into the mirror and recite these words:

*'I will learn the secrets
of the soul
I am one with the
eternal Universe
I am connected with all
greatness and genius.'*

WHAT I THINK, I BECOME

The Travel Spell

For this Spell you will need these ingredients:

★

one or two travel brochures containing pictures of the places you'd like to visit

one or two clippings of holiday and travel packages

a mirror (a wall mirror or dressing-table mirror is best)

some sticky tape

a green pen or crayon

If you'd like to travel the world or go away for a great holiday, cast this Spell on the first Monday of the month.

Gather the Spell ingredients together and go to a private room where you can be alone for at least half an hour.

Place the brochures and travel clippings on a flat surface and choose your favourite destination. Hold that clipping in your hand and repeat these words:

'With the wings of
Mercury
With freedom I fly —
So Let It Be.'

Now stick the clipping face down on the mirror with the sticky-tape and on then write on the side facing you the number seven.

Close your eyes and breathe evenly and deeply for a minute or two while you concentrate on your wish to travel. Fill yourself with carefree happy thoughts and tell yourself how much you deserve to have this vacation.

Leave the clippings up on the mirror for at least twelve days and every time you walk past think of how you will be feeling once you are on vacation, relaxing and having a great time.

The Friendship Spell

For this Spell you will need these ingredients:

★

three pieces of cotton or woollen yarn about 30 cms (12 ins) in length: the first red, the second blue and the third white

three feathers (any type)

All of us desire to be loved and respected. Friends are important, and loyal ones are hard to find. This Spell is wonderful for enhancing current relationships or ushering new friends into your life.

Cast your Spell on the evening of a New Moon, and remember: *you* are your own best friend first, and 'to have a friend is to be a friend'.

Plait or braid the three pieces of thread together while you repeat these words:

'Thread of the red, blue and white, Weave your Magic Spell tonight.'

Now take the three feathers and tie the stalks of the feathers onto your colourful braid. They should be tied at evenly spaced intervals. Then repeat these words:

Then tie the braid around your wrist to make a Magic bracelet. Whether you'd like to strengthen an existing friendship or find a new friend, touch one feather at a time and make your wish.

'Thread of the red,
blue and white,
Weave your Magic
Spell tonight.
All that I desire bring
When I touch these
feathers and this
string.
Cast this Spell and
make it true,
One for white, for red
and blue.'

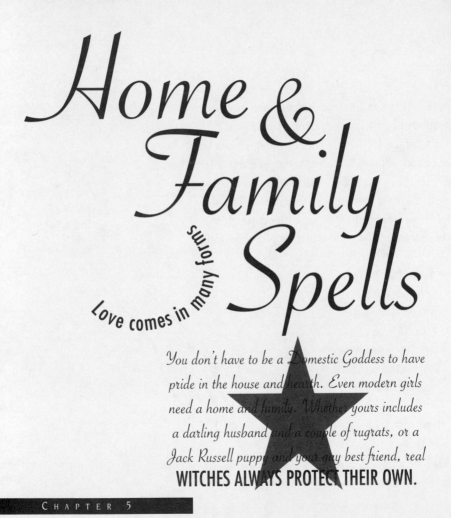

Home & Family Spells

Love comes in many forms

You don't have to be a Domestic Goddess to have pride in the house and hearth. Even modern girls need a home and family. Whether yours includes a darling husband and a couple of rugrats, or a Jack Russell puppy and your gay best friend, real **WITCHES ALWAYS PROTECT THEIR OWN.**

The Magic Lock Spell

For this Spell you will need these ingredients:

★

a long scarf

a baby's rattle

a wooden stick

seven small stones

The best time to cast this Spell is on the night of a Full Moon.

As the night commences, wait until you can be alone or undisturbed in your home. Drape the scarf around your shoulders and repeat the following chant:

'With this Magic cloak the Spell begins.'

The next thing is to take the baby rattle in one hand and the wooden stick in the other hand, and walk through every room in your home as you repeat the following words aloud:

'With the shake
of the rattle,
With the stroke
of the wand,
Let all unhappiness
be gone.'

After you have done
this, put down the
rattle and stick, and
pick up the seven
small stones. Close
your eyes for a minute
or two. Focus your
mind on positive
energy flowing towards
you, and imagine that
the stones in your
hands are becoming
warm and energised.
Then put your Magic
stones near the front
and the back door of
your home (preferably
where they won't be
seen).

Home Sweet Home Spell

For this Spell you will need these ingredients:

some lavender

a teaspoon of dried violet leaves or seven fresh ones

some grass clippings

some wood shavings

seven small paper bags

seven purple ribbons or pieces of thread

a purple pen or crayon

The best time to cast this Spell is at nine o'clock in the morning or evening.

Put all these items on a table. Place a teaspoon of each ingredient in each of the seven bags. Tie up each bag with a purple ribbon, and then draw a five-pointed star on each of the bags. Hold one of the bags in both hands and raise it above your head while you repeat these words:

'Lavender and violet,
Grass and wood,
Make my home as safe
as it should.'

Now find seven places in the cupboards and drawers of your home where the bags can be left undisturbed for at least three months.

You can repeat this Spell as often as you wish.

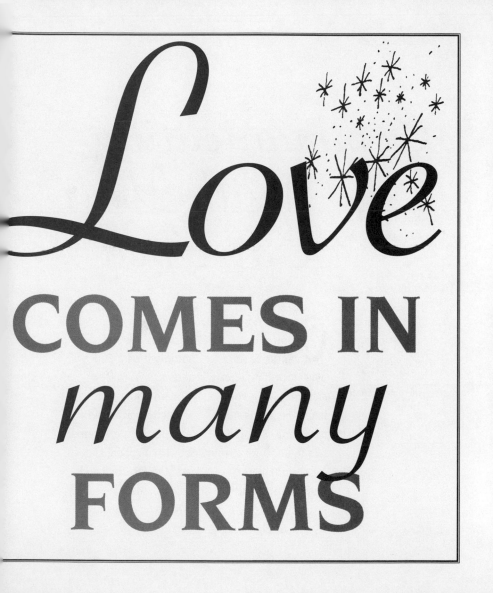

Communicating With Your Cat Spell

For this Spell you will need these ingredients:

★

some aniseeds

a mortar and pestle or a wooden bowl and spoon

a teaspoon of rosemary

a small amount of valerian tea leaves

a small cheesecloth square

a blue ribbon

Cats have been known for centuries as psychic and mystical creatures, and your family moggy is no exception. If you'd like to know what your cat is thinking or perhaps bring him into your Magic circle, try this Spell.

The best time to cast this Spell is at midnight on a Full Moon.

Grind the aniseeds with either a mortar and pestle or a wooden bowl and spoon, and add the rosemary and valerian tea leaves. While you're mixing, recite these words:

'By the eye of the cat,
By the wing of the bat,
Be clean and clear,
Bring his [or her]
spirit near.'

Place the mixture in a cheesecloth bag and tie it up with the ribbon. Wear this bag in your pocket when you're around your puddytat.

Protection Oil Spell

For this Spell you will need these ingredients:

★

two white candles

three sandalwood incense sticks

a teaspoon of red wine

three blades of grass

a cup, quarter-full of olive oil

This protection Spell is one of the oldest Enchantments and has been used for centuries to protect and bring love into the family home.

The best time to cast this Spell is on a Friday.

Put all these items on a table, and seat yourself comfortably in a chair. Light the candles and the incense sticks. Then relax your body and mind for a few minutes. Put the red wine and the three blades of grass into the olive oil, and pick up the cup in both hands while you recite these words:

'By the power of
the earth,
By the life in
the blade,
Be thou protected —
So Mote It Be.'

Sprinkle a few drops of the Protection Oil onto a clean cloth and wipe over the front door and the back door of your home.

Healthy Family Spell

For this Spell you will need these ingredients:

★

a wooden spoon

a china bowl

some mint

a clove

some grated lemon peel

a bay leaf

some rosehips

a cotton or muslin handkerchief

a red ribbon

To help protect your household from colds and flu, try this ancient Spell.

The best time to cast this Spell is on a Sunday.

Use the wooden spoon to mix all the ingredients together

in the bowl, while you recite this chant:

*'I conjure thee to be a protection,
I invoke the Magic of old,
To keep my family healthy and well —
So Mote It Be.'*

Place all the mixture onto the handkerchief and tie up the ends with the ribbon. Hang the healing pouch somewhere in your home.

CHAPTER 6

The Rest of Your Life Spells

You create your own destiny

MAGIC IS A SCIENCE. *It is a combination of technology and emotion which can be used to centre you, bring your desires into focus and improve all areas of your life.*

The physical world is only a small part of our Universe — if you imagine your thoughts as electrical energy, you can learn to channel your willpower to achieve any number of things.

Create Your Own Destiny Spell

For this Spell you will need these ingredients:

★

a dressing gown or bathrobe (preferably one you use only for Magical ceremonies)

a mirror

two white candles

a green apple cut in half

a cucumber cut in half

a piece of paper

a pen

The best time to cast this Spell is on a Sunday.

Begin by taking a bath or shower, then get dressed in your ceremonial gown. Gather all the items of Enchantment on a flat surface but near the mirror, so that when you sit down you can see your reflection. Light the candles. Pick up the apple and the cucumber, and breathe in a few deep breaths. Focus your thoughts on what you'd like to achieve in the future. Think big, and write down your ideas on the piece of paper.

Look into the mirror and repeat these words:

'I will travel from the depth to the light,
I am my own Universe — capable of all things,
I create my own Destiny.'

Read out the ideas you've written down, and add the words: 'I will do this — this is my future'.

Psychic Development Spell

For this Spell you will need only one ingredient:

★

your imagination

This Spell will help you develop your psychic abilities and should be done as often as possible to exercise your mind power.

Find a private place where you can be undisturbed, and seat yourself in a comfortable position. Close your eyes, and do some deep breathing for a minute or two. Allow your whole being to relax completely, and if any negative or confused thoughts come in to your mind, breathe through them until you feel at peace and are clear minded.

Open your eyes and hold both of your

hands in front of you. Imagine that you are holding a ball — perhaps the size of an orange — in your hands. Imagine how the ball itself physically feels, and focus on its roundness and size. After you have a good sense of the ball, imagine that it's turning into the colour red and it's getting warmer, then it's blue and it's getting cooler. Then thrown the ball lightly into the air and catch it, feel its weight against your hands. Put the ball slowly down in front of you to seal and finish the Spell.

The Nature Spell

For this Spell you will need these ingredients:

★

some clean, simple clothes made of any natural fibre

a long piece of thread or string

The old expression 'knock on wood' comes from the Druids who would knock on the oak tree to say hello to the tree spirit.

This Enchantment will help centre and heal you of any nervous tension.

The best time to cast this Spell is at midday.

Put on the clothes of natural fibre. Find a healthy looking tree and wrap the string around it. Sit down on the ground and recite these words:

'O *great tree*,
O *strong tree*,
Give me your healing
heart for this day.
O *great tree*,
O *strong tree*,
Heal me my heart,
Blessed Be.'

Now wrap your arms
around the tree trunk
and give it a big hug.
Put your face up
against the bark, and
try to feel the lifeforce
filling you with healing
energy.

When you feel
energised, take off the
string and roll it up in
a ball. Take it with you
for good luck.

When it's Time to Say Goodbye Spell

For this Spell you will need these ingredients:

★

your favourite clothes

a little make-up

a mirror

an egg

two white candles

some rosemary

some chamomile

There are times when we know the relationship is well and truly over, but we just can't seem to let go. This Spell will help heal an aching heart and get you back on track in no time.

The best time to cast this Spell is on a Saturday at five o'clock in the evening.

Take a bath or shower and then get

dressed in your favourite clothes. Put on a little make-up, and seat yourself in front of your mirror. Put the items of Enchantment in front of you, on a table or flat surface. Light the candles, and sprinkle some of the rosemary and chamomile around you. Take a few deep, relaxing breaths. Then hold the egg lightly in one hand and repeat this chant:

'I *now let go of all unhappiness and heartache,* I *receive love from the Universe,* And I *deserve love and inner peace.'*

Keep looking in the mirror and roll the egg lightly over your forehead and imagine sending all negative thoughts and feelings into the egg.

Then throw the egg into the garbage.

I CREATE MY

DESTINY

The Crystal Singer Spell

For this Spell you will need these ingredients:

★

a white candle

a peridot crystal

Did you know that crystals can feel your energy? Scientists are just now beginning to understand the incredible aspects of crystals, but Magicians have always known that crystals sing with power.

This Spell will help you project your speaking voice so you can communicate to others more clearly.

The best time to cast this Spell is at eight o'clock in the morning or evening.

Light the candle, then hold the crystal in your hand and recite this chant:

'Ah Oh My.'

Keep chanting this until it sounds like singing. Feel the crystal getting warm in your hands, and imagine your voice is flowing through the crystal.

The Beautiful Body Spell

With so much obsession about weight in today's world, it's no wonder that many of us have times when we feel as if we should lose a few pounds. Getting stuck into the chockies and stacking on excessive weight can mean that you feel the need to comfort and protect yourself from the outside world — it's just like putting on a suit of armour. Instead of fighting these feelings, go with them and look to understand the cause of your fears. Voluptuous curves are not the real issue here. You only have to look at how society constantly changes in what it considers beauty. Don't be a slave to the opinions of others — you are beautiful as you are.

For this Spell you will need these ingredients:

★

a recording of soothing music

some perfume

your favourite, perfumed body oil or gel

some henna powder

a small paintbrush

a necklace

an ankle bracelet

This Spell will help you feel and project a better body image and, lo and behold, amazing things will follow.

The best time to cast this Spell is at seven o'clock in the morning or evening.

Make some time for yourself when you can

take a long and luxurious bath or shower. Dry yourself, go into your bedroom, soften the lights, and play some soothing music. Start to anoint you body with the perfume and the oil. Take your time, stroking each part of your body, feeling the sensation of your soft skin. Mix a little henna powder with water, and paint a red dot on your forehead and a star on each palm of your hands. Put on the necklace and ankle bracelet, and stand in front of your mirror, with your palms facing outwards, and repeat these Magic words:

'Mirror mirror on the wall
Who's the fairest of them all?
I am — and my body is my sacred temple.'

Cast this Spell as often as you like.

Wishes Come True Spell

This Spell is an interactive Enchantment in which you can join with Athena and Deborah's Bellthane energy to help you manifest your greatest wishes.

The best time to cast this Spell is on the eve of a New Moon.

Each symbol has been charged with Magic. Choose the symbol that most appeals to you, and place your index finger on top to activate it.

Now imagine that a golden light is surrounding you, and feel the symbol becoming warm and full of power.

Speak your wish out loud and follow with these words:

'I am a child of love,
The Oracle loves me
And sends me all I need.'

To be most effective, no-one but you should make a wish with your chosen symbol.

Magic is Everywhere Spell

For this Spell you might like to have the following ingredient, but it is optional:

★

a crystal

Where are the best places to perform Magic? In forests, ruins, mountaintops, caves and deserts, beside lightning-struck trees, near standing stones and ancient monuments, on seashores, by the banks of great streams, at a crossroads.

But let's be practical — your own home can always be used with great results. It is after all your powerbase, and it's where you can be entirely yourself.

If someone asks you 'Where do I find Magic?', you can now answer 'Where is Magic not?' Magic is in everything and everybody, and you can connect with its power even at the local supermarket or at a noisy club.

This Spell will open up the psychic realm wherever you are.

You can hold a crystal while you're casting the Spell if you like, but it's not completely necessary. Take a few deep breaths, and adjust your back and spine so you feel your energy flow more evenly. Feel a sense of openness. Imagine there is a waterfall of white light showering over you and filling you with energy. Now the light is wrapping around you and becoming like a cocoon. Let the cone of white light massage you, and imagine that you are changing into a beautiful butterfly ready to fly from the cocoon back into the world.

Open your arms wide and allow the light to radiate from you, back out into the air, and filling everything around you with love and energy.

About the authors

ATHENA STARWOMAN was born into a long line of famous mystics. Her worldwide Press columns, features, television appearances, seminars and astrology work reveal her tremendous depth and understanding of the astrological and metaphysical realms. Athena's works are designed specifically to translate the ancient arts of astrology and other ancient mystical sciences into modern terms. In the USA she has written the *Vogue* Magazine horoscope for six years and began regular astrological columns for *Star* Magazine in 1994. Although Athena currently lives in New York, she remains very popular in Australia, where her column ran for twelve years in Sydney's *Mirror Telegraph* newspaper and still appears regularly in *Woman's Day*. 'My mission in this lifetime is to reawaken the psychic potential and mystical inheritance in others that has been ignored,' she says. 'We have forgotten the power our spiritual strength holds in today's world, and we must fight to reclaim it.'

DEBORAH GRAY has studied Celtic Magic and White Witchcraft for over twenty years, and was initiated by an Ancient Order with her Druid name, 'Bellthane', which aids her with the time-honoured wisdom of metaphysics. Like the universal image of the Muse, Deborah draws on her psychic studies for creative inspiration in her busy showbusiness career as a successful jazz singer and film actress. 'Magic has taught me to be fearless in both my work and in my spiritual life. In these frantic times people are looking for ways to bring harmony and achievement into their lives.' She has opened a psychic telephone service, 'Bellthane's Magic Psychic Line' and is the co-founder of the International Cosmic College. She is currently writing a mystical rock opera for film and television.